Ben is Gone Again

In Search of a Dog

GivinCuddles Books

Ben was a beautiful long-haired dog that enjoyed wandering the streets of Edson, Alberta before I met him. The first time I saw Ben, he was sitting on a concrete floor, behind a chain-link fence at the dog pound.

I just went there to look; I wasn't planning on taking a dog home, but then I saw Ben. He sat there so calm and quiet, his long nose pointed down, and his big brown eyes looking up at me. He reminded me, of the dog I used to watch on TV when I was a child.

As I drove home, I couldn't get him off my mind, and I just had to have him! By the time I got home, the dog pound was already closed, so I had to wait till the next day.

The next morning I called the dog pound, and told the lady on the phone that I wanted the collie. My joy slipped away when she said Ben was on his way to a rescue organization, an hour's drive away. She gave me their phone number, and I quickly gave them a call. I explained to the lady on the phone what had happened, and I told her that I was on my way to pick Ben up. I asked her to tell me how to find her place.

She said she had to go to the veterinary clinic, and asked me to meet her there. When I arrived at the clinic, she was the only one there, so I introduced myself and immediately, she said, "He's gone." I was shocked; I couldn't believe what I was hearing.

As I stood there in silence, she suggested that I should take a look at the other dogs at her place. I didn't have the courage to tell her that I didn't drive all that way to look for just any dog. I only wanted Ben, but I followed her back to her place in the country anyway.

As I drove down the long gravel road, I said, "God, in Jesus name, if you want me to have Ben, please help us to find him before I leave here, because I don't want to have to drive all the way back here again."

When we arrived at her place, she took me over to where she kept all the dogs that needed a home.

We weren't there long and her cell phone rang. It was her friend, telling her about a stray dog she saw. She quickly walked towards her truck and said, "I'm going to see if it's Ben, I'll be right back."

It wasn't long before her truck came bouncing up the driveway again. I looked and was delighted to see that Ben was with her! I quickly opened the door of my vehicle as she brought him over. He eagerly jumped into my truck while wagging his tail; I patted him on the head and quickly shut the door. I followed her into the house to fill out some papers as fast as I could, and hurried out again. I jumped into my red truck, thanked God, and headed home!

What should have been a ten-minute drive to the dog pound to pick up Ben turned out to be a very long and emotional day. I was happy to finally have Ben, and he looked happy as he stared out the window on the long drive home.

I pulled into the yard, closed the gate behind me, and let Ben out.

He ran around sniffing, and then flopped over and rolled on the grass.

He dug a small hole
in the cool sand
and laid down.

I invited him into the house, and after looking around, he settled down on the living room floor. I left him in the house and went to the garage to take my other dog Caleb outside to tie him up, so he could safely meet Ben.

I put a leash on Ben and took him over to see Caleb. Their noses met and they calmly sniffed each other, so I untied them and let them play.

They spent many days playing together and running through the trees before the snow fell. They seemed to enjoy the cooler weather and found a stick that neither one of them was willing to let go of.

And they pulled.

Then they took turns rolling in the fluffy snow while wrestling.

Ben sat in the snow, listening for a mouse.

Ben waited for Caleb to join him.

They heard a mouse and dove into the snow together.

Caleb got tired of hunting and found a toy to play with, while Ben tried to take it from him.

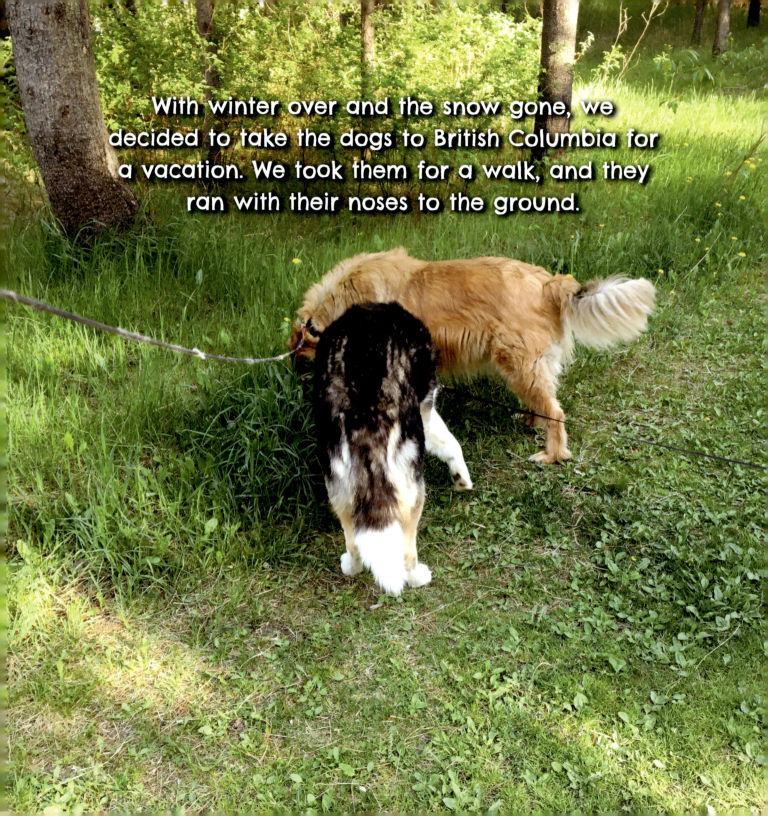

With winter over and the snow gone, we decided to take the dogs to British Columbia for a vacation. We took them for a walk, and they ran with their noses to the ground.

The water was cold, so Ben decided to come out. We put the dogs in the van and drove up the highway to Nakusp.

It was a warm summer day, and after exploring Nakusp, Ben carefully stepped into the water at Upper Arrow Lake, while Caleb watched the people in the distance.

The dogs rested comfortably in the van as we drove.

After a long day in the van, Ben and Caleb were happy to be in their own back yard again.

Ben loves us,
and we love him.

The end.

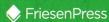

Suite 300 - 990 Fort St
Victoria, BC, V8V 3K2
Canada

www.friesenpress.com

Copyright © 2020 by GivinCuddles Books
First Edition — 2020

books.givincuddles@gmail.com

All rights reserved.

No part of this publication may be reproduced in any form, or by any means, electronic or mechanical, including photocopying, recording, or any information browsing, storage, or retrieval system, without permission in writing from FriesenPress.

ISBN
978-1-5255-6964-7 (Hardcover)
978-1-5255-6965-4 (Paperback)
978-1-5255-6966-1 (eBook)

1. JUVENILE NONFICTION, ANIMALS, DOGS

Distributed by GivinCuddles Books

Printed in Canada